The words of

A Not So Normal Woman.

"You're ridiculous."
"Maybe. But you still love me."
"Like a mad woman loves her slippers and whiskey."

I know you.

You'll take the chance.

You'd rather be dead on the inside after feeling completely alive, than being half numb and never knowing if you could have had it all.

Take off your shoes
and get back in the sand.
It's just dirt.
It'll wash off
when you get
to where you're going.

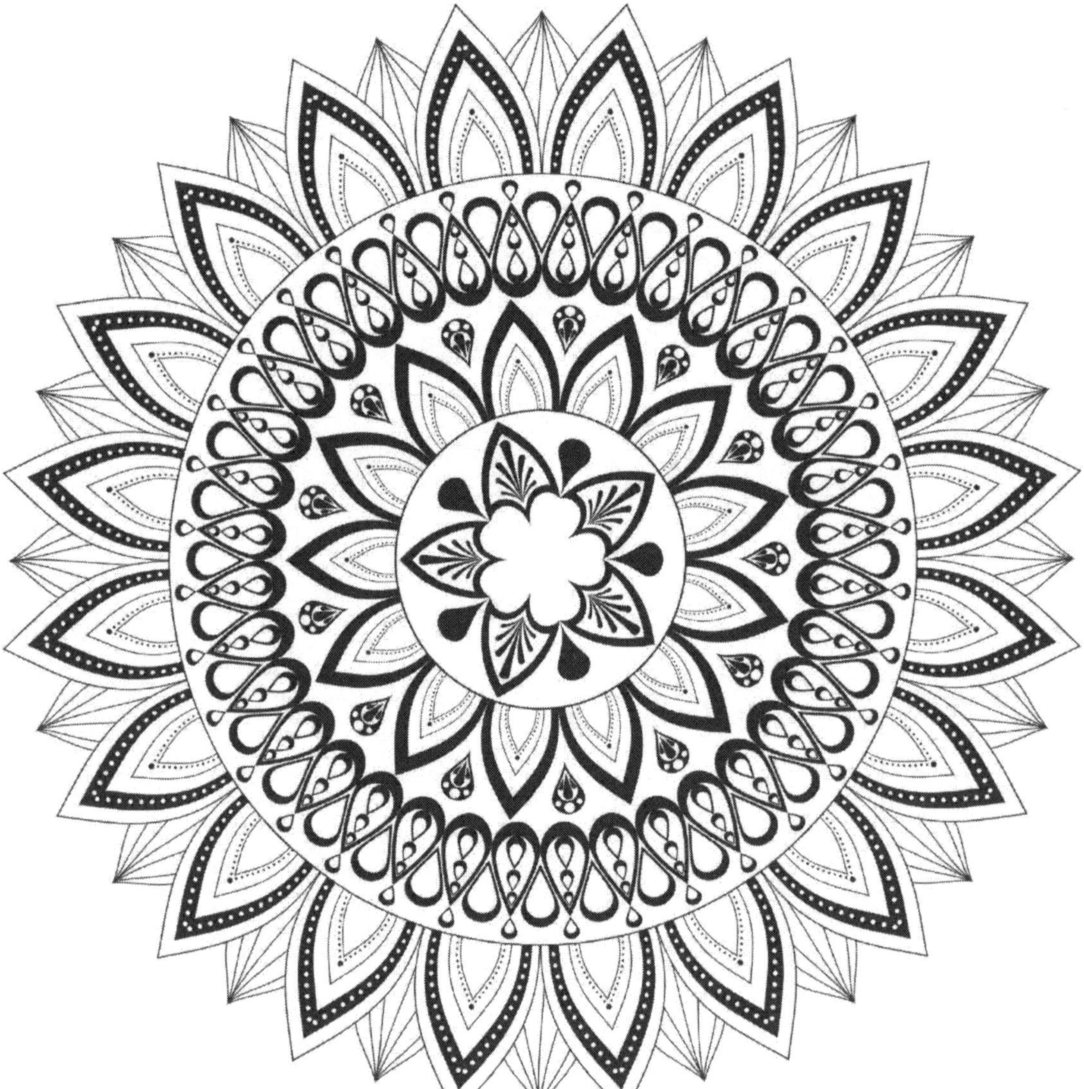

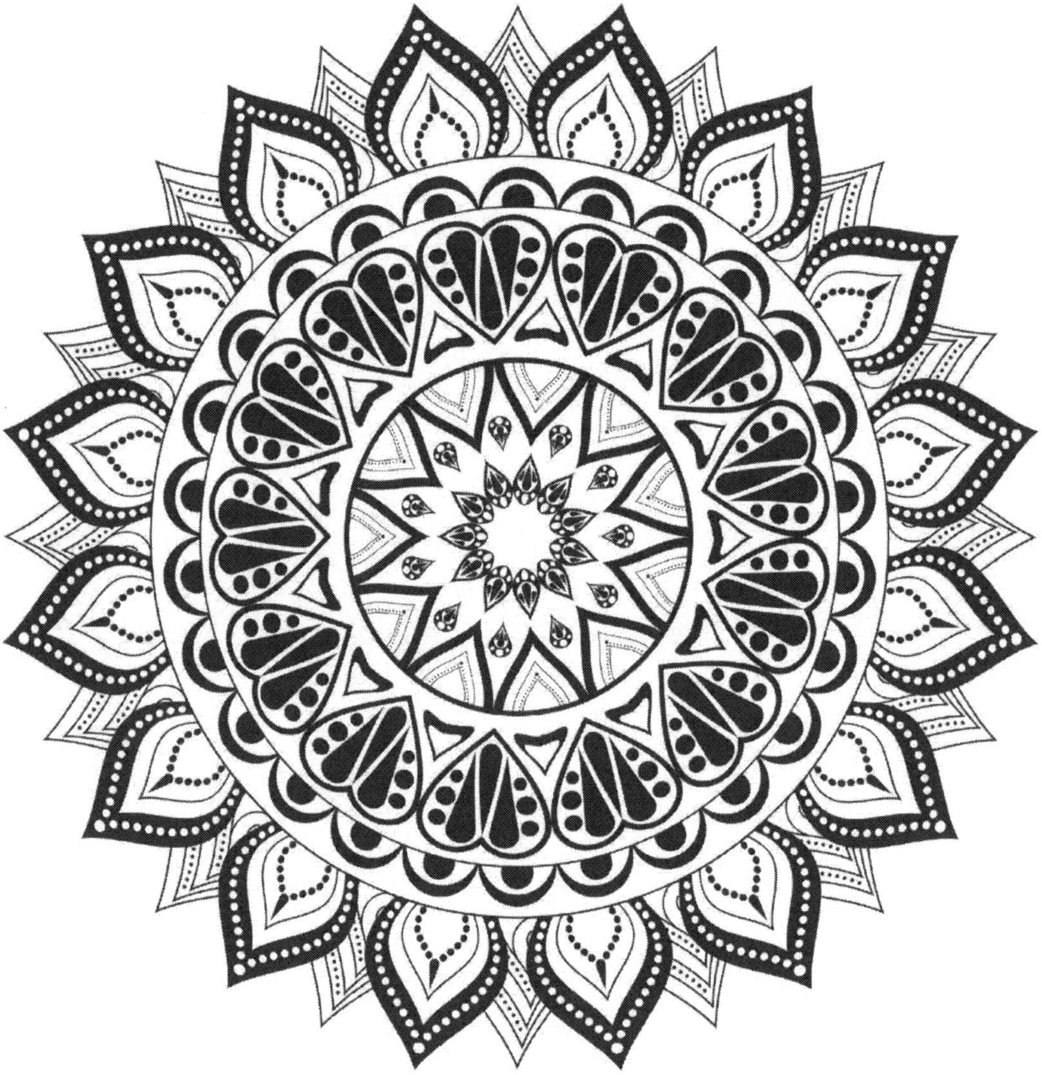

"You want some tea or something?"

"Tea?"

"Is that not what people drink in a crisis?"

"You're thinking of Tequila."

Personally,
I've always hated structure
and plans.
Security or not.
People don't belong in boxes.

"I'm guessing he could use some of your kindness and compassion. Your unwavering love and your sick sense of humor... to name a few of your most admirable assets."

"How can you be so sure?"

"Because everyone needs more of those."

"I don't know. Everything was great this morning. Then, you got all in my head!"

"Yeah, I do that. Like to get in there and really rearrange shit if I can."

Thanks for being the sort of friend who gets drunk and parades around in her prom dress at three in the morning.

Regardless of how
ridiculous she acts;
she expects to be taken seriously.
Apparently,
it's part of the best friend code.
I just take her word for it.
That's part of the code, too.

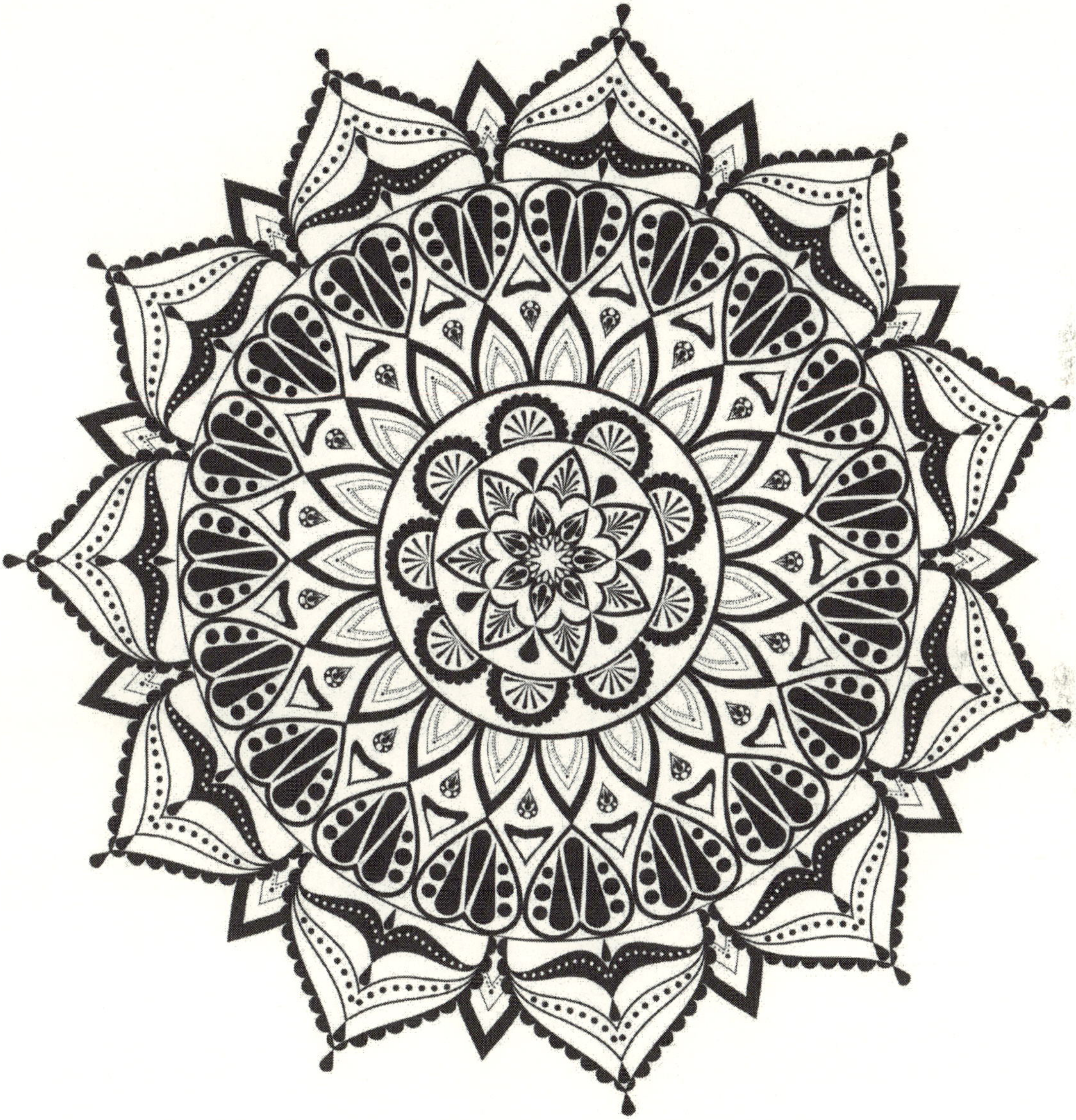

You want to
bring something
to the table?
Bring yourself.
That's all anyone
wants anyway.

You need therapy in such a big way.

"I feel like our friendship is on very shaky ground right now."

"Get real. When has either one of us ever known solid ground?"

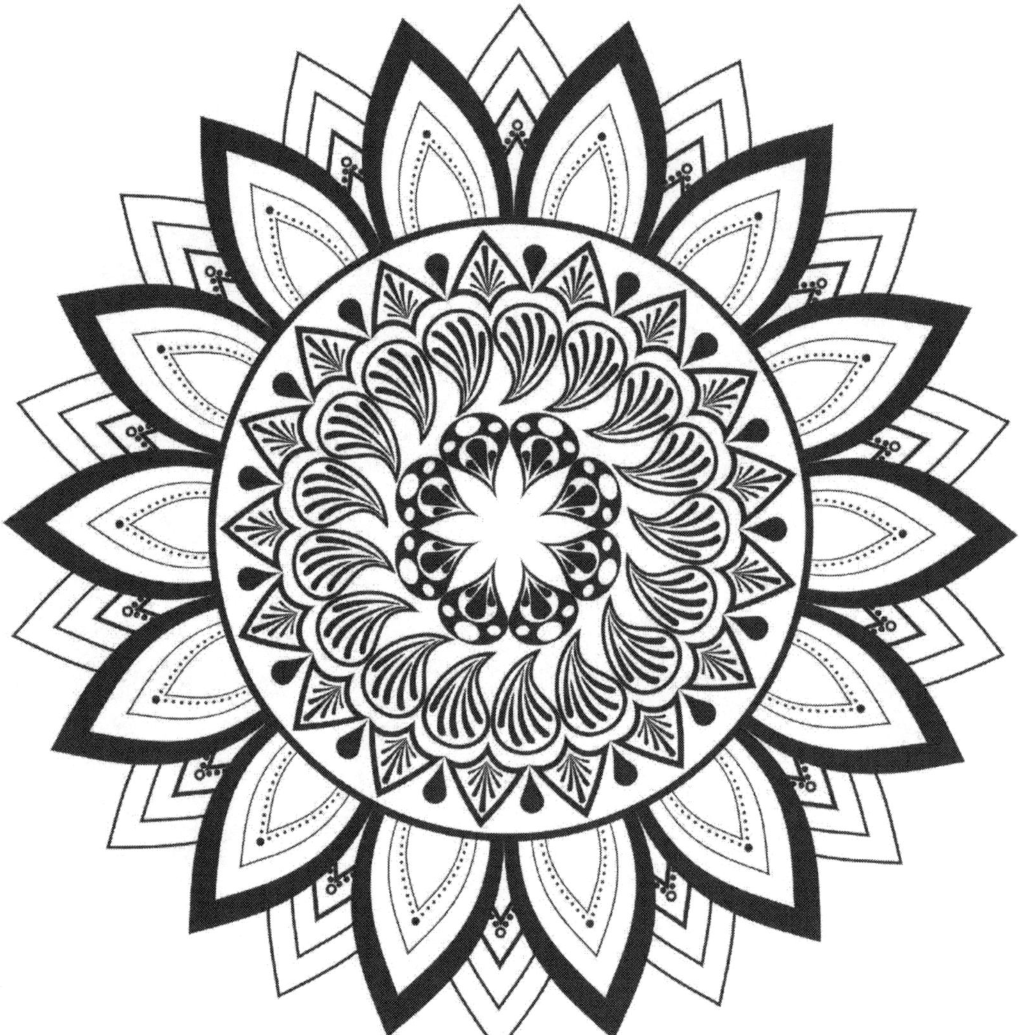

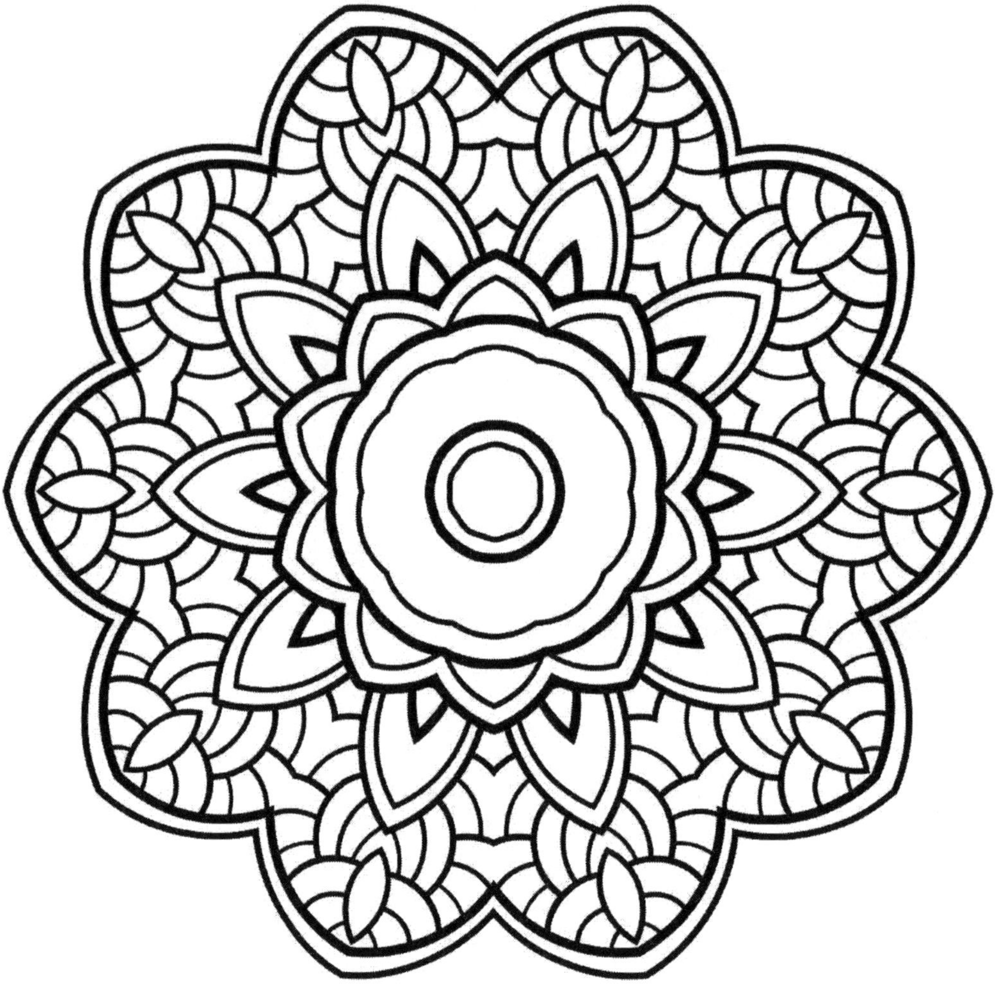

I'm a splendid friend.

I see you

for all your fabulous faults

and I love you not despite them,

but because of.

Mostly, I'm just trying not to think anything for the time being. Figured if I just let it all simmer for a bit, the important shit would float to the top, you know?

"I have cake."

"I could eat cake.

I could eat a lot of it."

I like this dress.
It's my 'I want to
eat cake' dress.

Since when don't you have anything to offer? Have you met you?

Every chick should be the hero
of her own story.
I'm not saying she can't have a man
by her side when she saves the day.
I'm not even saying the guy can't save it.
I'm just saying he doesn't save her.
Nobody can save anybody except themselves.
Trust me on this.
There's no perk to being the dimwitted virgin.
You get treated like an idiot
and you never get laid.

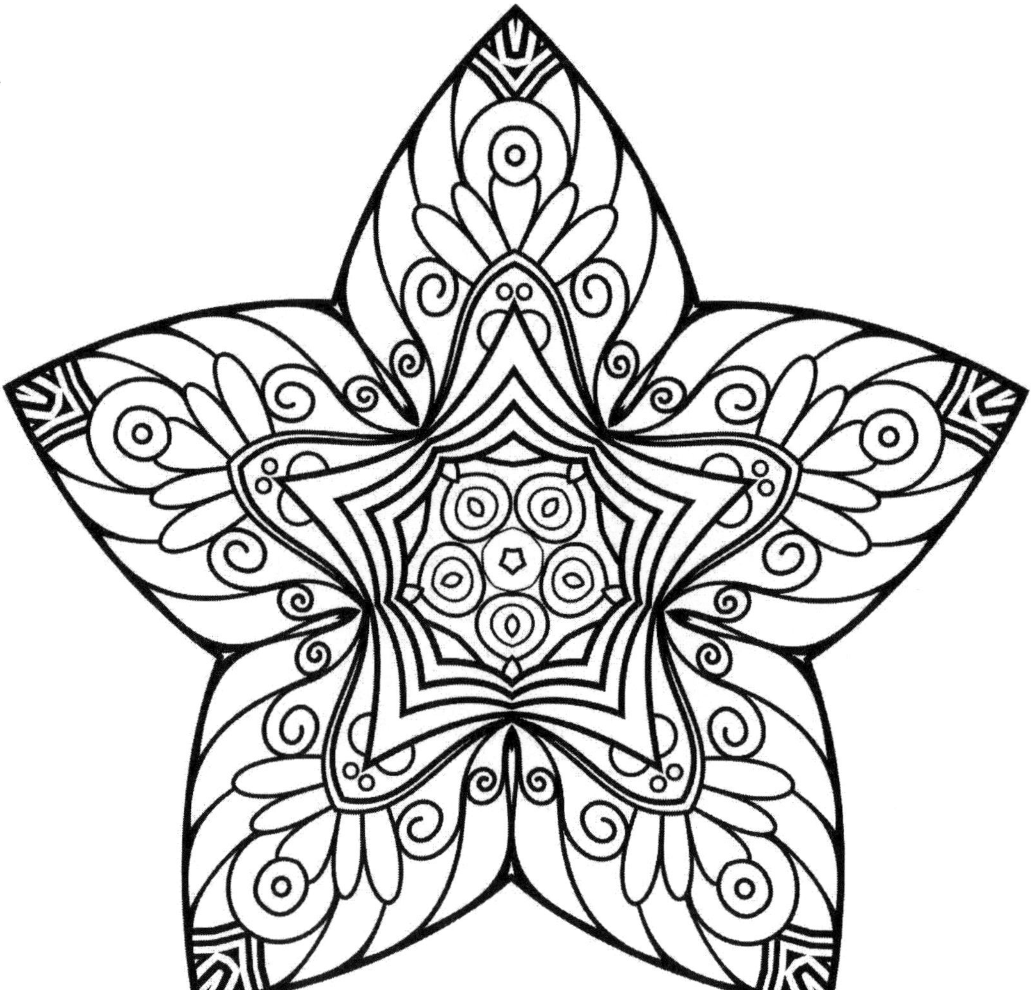

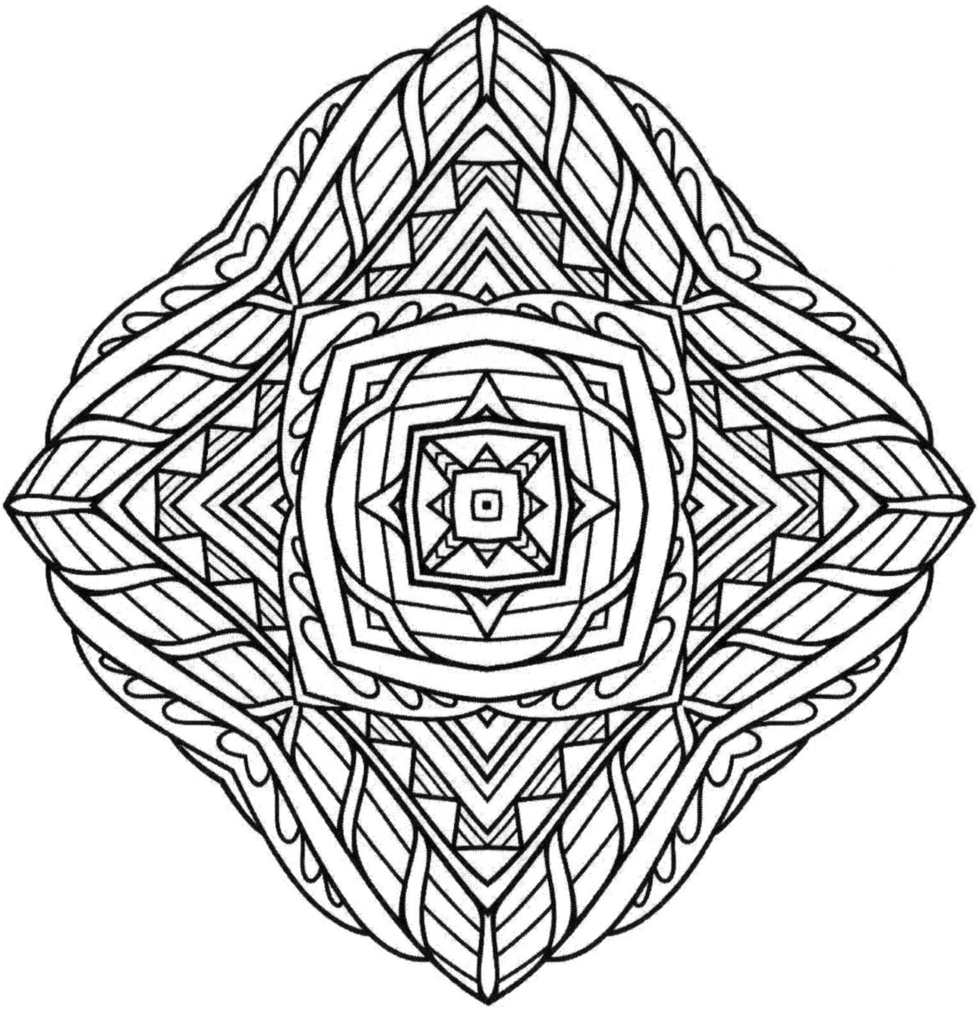

What made you change your mind?
It was my awesome insight wasn't it?

There are moments

my head wants to explode

just hearing some of the asinine

things you say to push people's buttons

and there are others

when my heart swells

with gratitude

just knowing you're my friend.

If you're not going to take my candy,
I guess you're going to be stuck
taking my advice.
It's good shit,
but it's not nearly as enjoyable as chocolate.
So, keep that in mind
next time you're in an emotional pickle
and I come wandering along.

"Not every problem can be solved with chocolate."

"Wrong. Name one problem you've had I haven't fixed with chocolate."

Feeding you chocolate
and making you laugh
when life is too hard to cry,
that's my thing.
It's what you come here for.

Brief moments of trivial life crap will help balance out the heavy shit you're going to be trudging through for a long while to come.

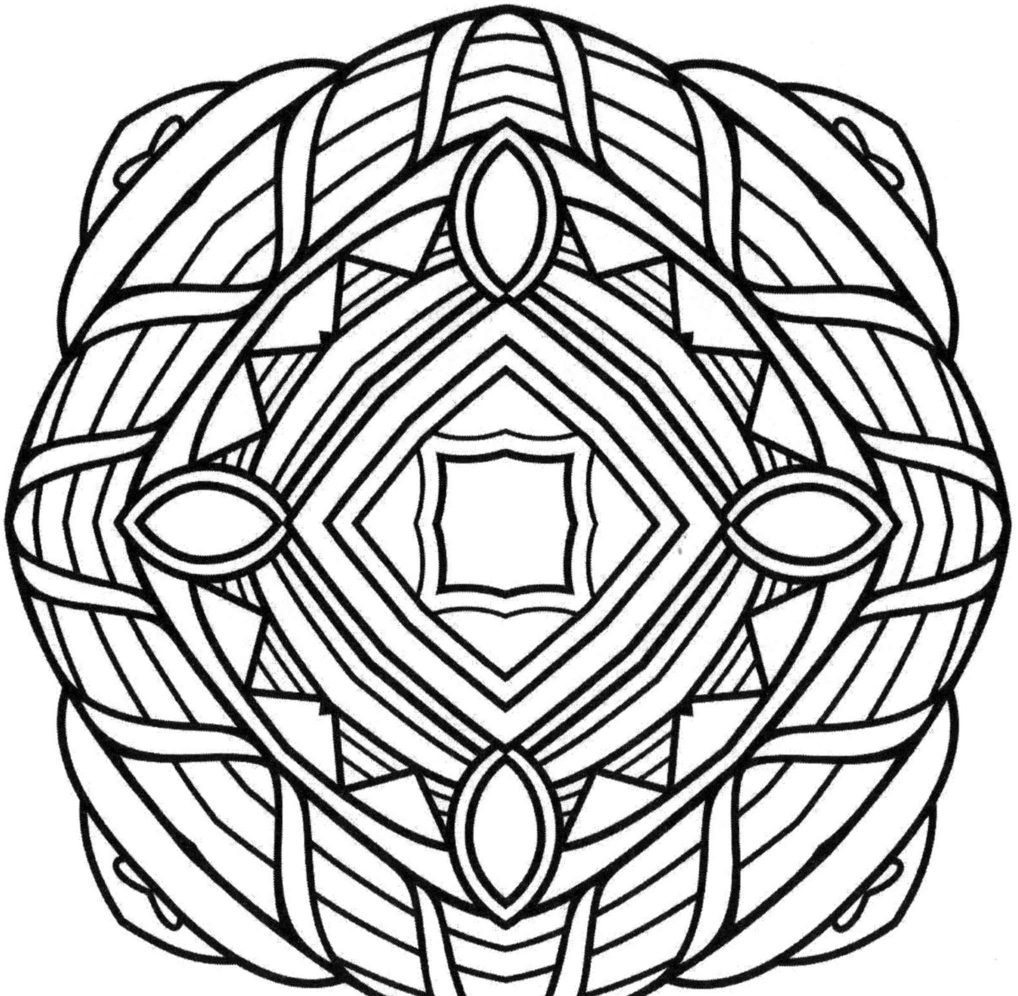

"I so appreciate you bringing up the most traumatic moments of my life when I'm already hanging on by the last strip of my sanity."

"Don't be ridiculous. You haven't had a scrap of sanity to cling to since before I met you."

I bet you've got hidden talents you've never even dreamed of.

Yeah, okay.
You keep telling yourself that.
When you're ready
to hear some more honest shit,
you let me know.
I'll tell ya some.

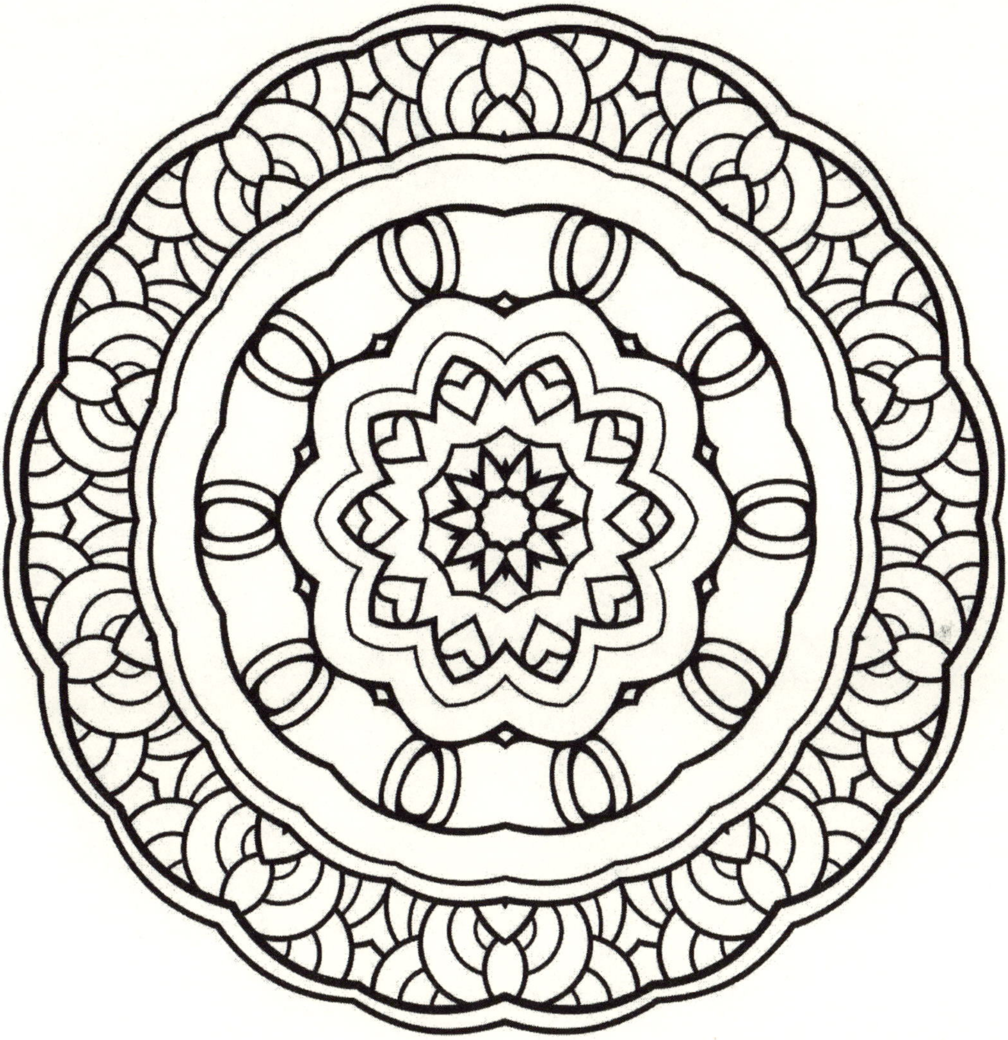

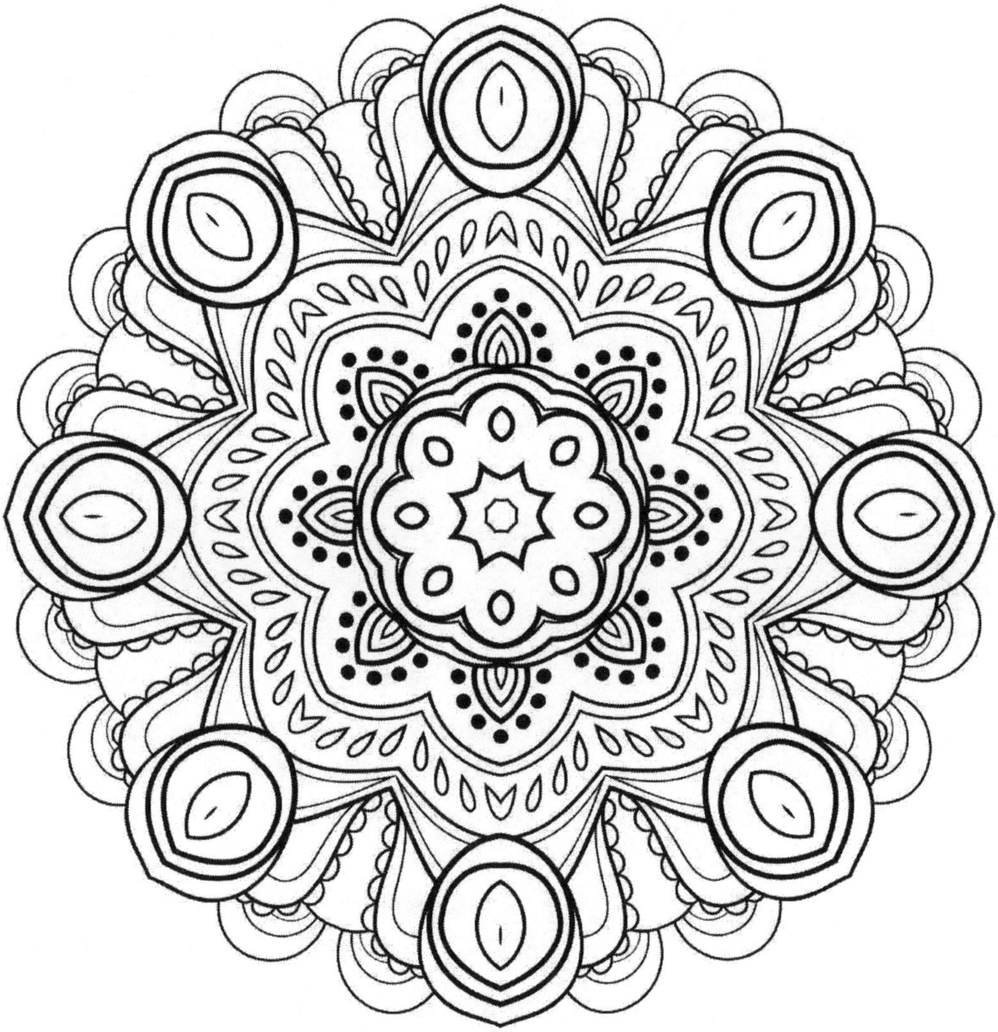

Just treat her like any other wild animal. Keep calm, don't run and for the love of GOD, do not make eye contact. It will only encourage her.

Only three possible slots
for men to land in.
Family.
Soulmate.
Or, just a speck of dust
on the road of your life.

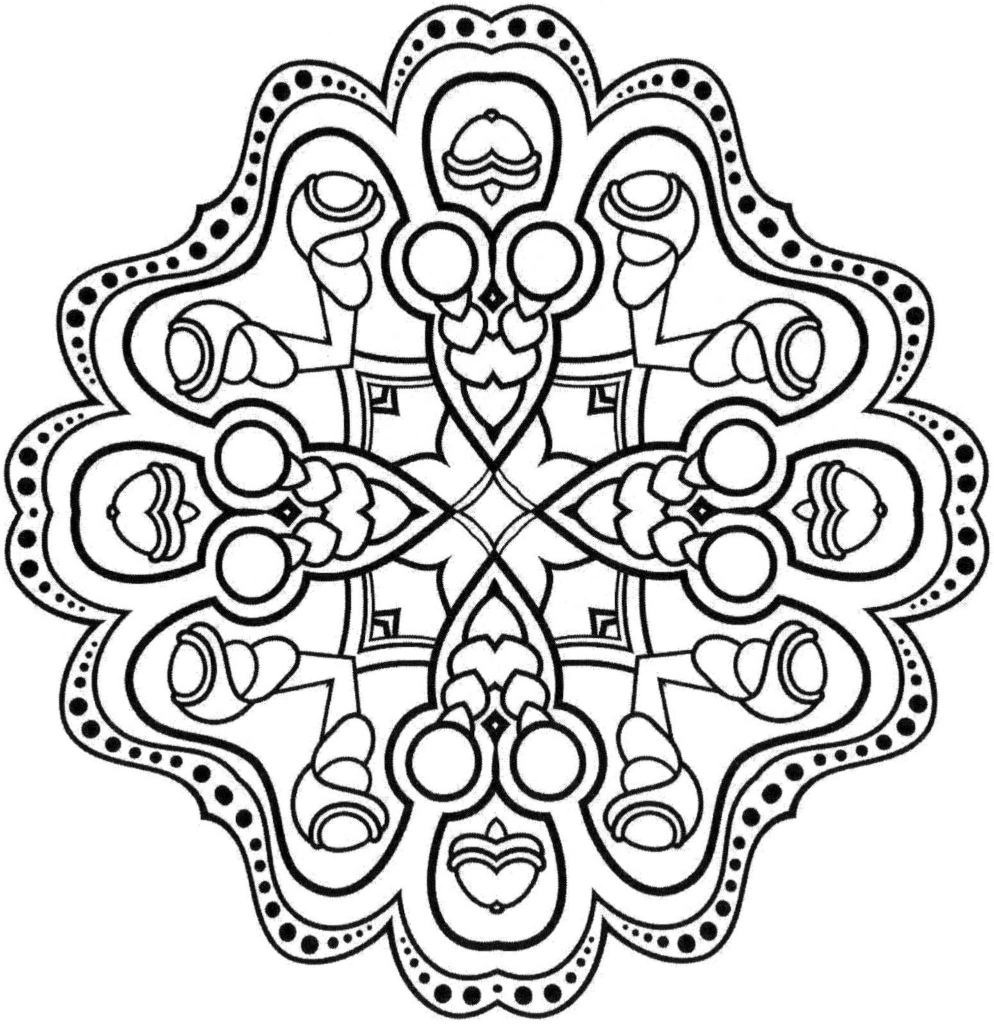

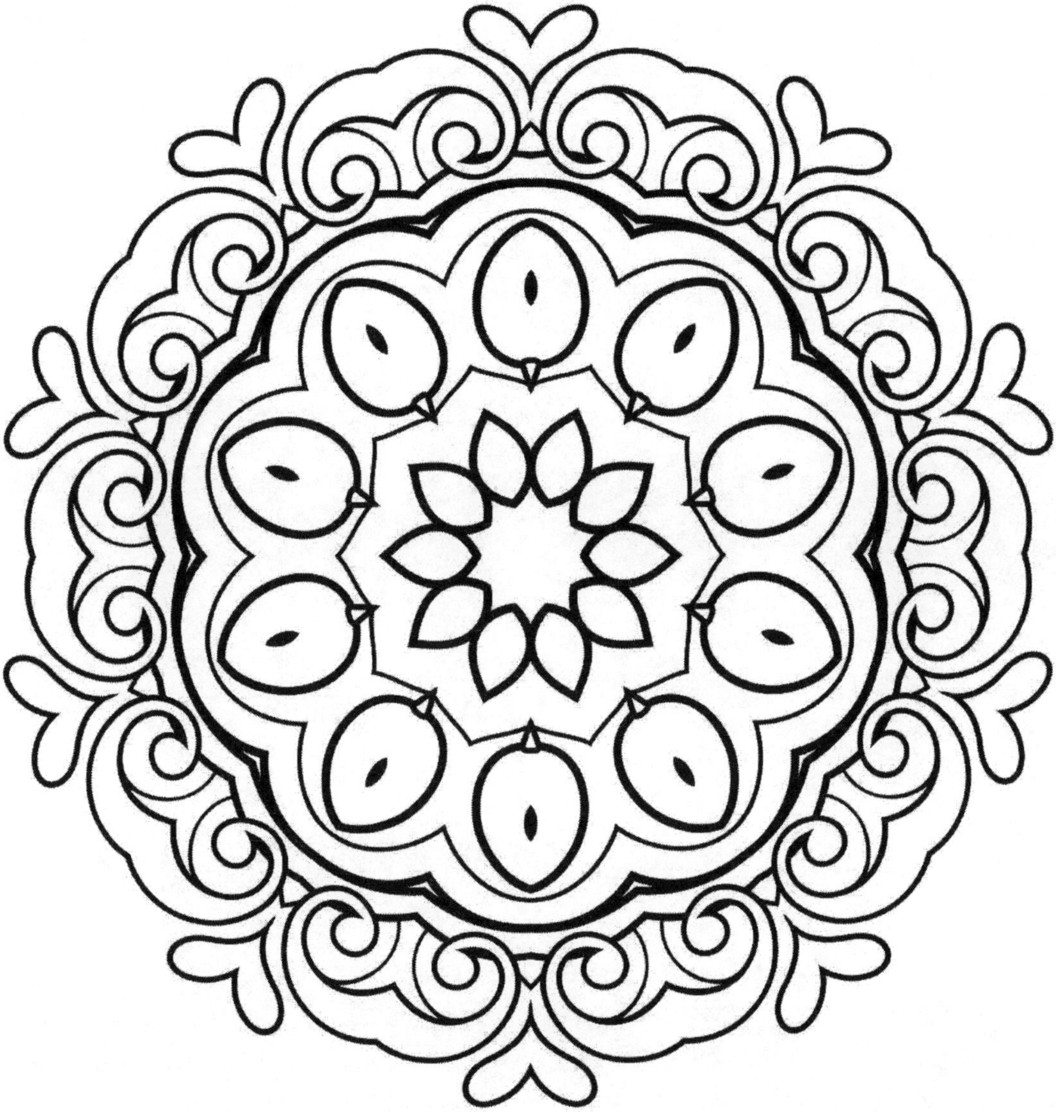

Here you are,
doubting yourself and too scared
to leave the path laid out before you.
The familiar one.
The one guaranteed to deliver
a sound success.
Fuck that.
Stop being so scared of your own talent.
Stop waiting for someone to come along
and push you off that path a second time.
You're not a fucking baby bird.
You already know how to fly.

A SheJournals Journal published by Wild Girl Art

Copyright © 2019 - by K.S. Thomas aka Karina Giörtz
www.authorksthomas.com

All writing provided by K.S. Thomas (aka Karina Giörtz)

Most quotes can be found in the following novels –

With Whom We Spend Our Lives
Don't Fall
Nine
Forget Me Not
The Wild in Her Eyes
Ten
I call him Brady

Made in the USA
Columbia, SC
30 November 2022